BOATING LIFE AND W
Poland's River Odra in the 1950s

Milepost Research
2001

The Masurian Lakes are connected by small canals, some requiring locks to allow for a change in level. The lakes are heavily used by sailing and pleasure boats, with over 200 km of waterway available.

A passenger boat being hauled up one of the inclines on the Elbląg Canal, passing the second cradle which is descending. There are five inclines on the canal, and it takes a day for the trip from one end to the other.

© Mieczysław Wróblewski and Mike Clarke
All rights reserved.

ISBN 0-95192-361-7

British Library in Cataloguing Publication Data.
A catalogue record of this book is available from the British Library.

Published by: Milepost Research,
41 Fountain Street, Accrington, BB5 0QR

Poland's Waterways

As a political area, Poland's boundaries have been very 'flexible', at one time extending to take in most of today's Lithuania, Ukraine and Belarus, and in the eighteenth century declining until officially there was no such country as Poland. The one place where it has remained fixed is in the hearts of the Polish people – an example to us all in these days of worries about loss of national identity.

Poland, today, lies between the Oder in the west and reaches almost to the Niemen in the east, bounded by the Baltic Sea in the north and the Carpathian Mountains in the south. The ground slowly rises eastwards from the Oder until falling steeply into the valley of the Vistula and then slowly rising again to the valleys of the Niemen, Pripiat and Dnestr in the east.

Rivers, as elsewhere in Europe, were always used for carrying goods. Salt, from the internationally-renown Wieliczka mines, was carried by water as long ago as the thirteenth century. The main rivers used for navigation were the Oder and Vistula which carried north-south traffic; coal, metal and textiles on the former and grain and salt on the latter. The Noteć (Netze) and Warta took east-west traffic from the Oder, and the Bug from the Vistula.

Poland was divided in the late eighteenth century between the three great regional powers of the time – Prussia, Austria and Russia. Prussian took the area between Gdansk, Toruń and the Oder, and built the Bydgoszcz (Bromberg) Canal at this time to improve its trade with this new region. No doubt Frederick II saw the canal as a way of supplying his troops at the new frontier

A restored nineteenth century lock in a park on one of the disused canal sections in Bydgoszcz.

The underground canal at Zabrze from a drawing in the Coal Mining Museum.

with Russia. The canal was built between 1772 and 1774. It was 26km long and had ten locks. Eighty per cent of the half million tons carried annually in 1900 was timber. The canal was enlarged between 1905 and 1917 to allow boats of up to 400 tons carrying capacity to use the waterway, at which time the number of locks was reduced to six.

It was in the late eighteenth century that Prussia took over Silesia as well. They now controlled the whole of the Oder. The lower sections of the river had been improved in the early eighteenth century, with canals being built parallel to the river in some places. The first lock was opened in 1748 at Brzeg, others following at Oława and Wrocław later in the century. Frederick II saw the economic development of Silesia as vital, and English expertise was imported, particularly for the iron industry. The 46km long Kłodnice Canal linked the industrial area around Gliwice with the Oder at Koźle. Built between 1792 and 1812, it had 18 locks. The canal was rebuilt between 1934 and 1939 with just six locks and, on reopening, was called the Adolf Hitler Canal. Today it is better known as the Gliwice Canal.

There are two old locks in the centre of Wrocław on the Odra. They were taken out of service early in the twentieth century, but are now being restored for pleasure boats.

Between 1800 and 1806, a small canal was built from the coal mines at Zabrze and Gliwice which used two inclined planes. The canal entered the mines at Zabrze, and both the underground canal and the inclines were based on the underground canals at Worsley, on the Bridgewater Canal. The canal operated until 1834, closing because of problems with the coal strata at the mine.

Other rivers were improved, such as the Warta which serves Poznań, and the Vistula from Toruń to the important port of Gdańsk (Danzig). The division of Poland between Prussia and Russia effectively cut the Vistula in two, and only the lower section, in Prussian territory, was improved. (Subsequently, after the Second World War, locks were built on a section of the river around Kraków.) Much work was undertaken on improving the mouth of the river from Tczew to the sea in order to develop the port of Gdańsk. Export grain traffic was one of the most important cargoes.

Development of the high ground, or Oberland, to the east of the Vistula here was helped by the opening of the Elbląg (Oberland) Canal in 1860. Still in operation for pleasure boats, it has five inclined planes, four worked by water wheels

Left: The lock between the Vistula and the Nogat near Tczew. It was part of the flood protection measures taken to protect the low-lying land between the Vistula and Elbląg, the large dyke in the background holding back the waters of the Vistula during floods. A second smaller lock on the left allowed small boats to pass through a second dyke when the water level was at a suitable level.

Right: The Vistula above Toruń is still mostly unregulated. Despite this lack of improvement, the river was used by boats and rafts, but the conditions had to be right – neither too much nor too little water. Ice-breakers still patrol the river after the winter to stop the ice from damming up and thus causing flooding.

and one by a water turbine. The system was inspected by personnel from the Leeds & Liverpool Canal in the 1880s when they were looking for ways to improve their canal.

Canals were also built in the part of Poland under Russian control. The Augustowski Canal was built between 1824 and 1830 to carry agricultural products and timber for export, avoiding Prussian-controlled Gdańsk. Over 100km long, the section remaining in Poland (three locks are in Belarus) has been restored for pleasure boating. Outside of present-day Poland were the eighteenth century Oginski and Królewski canals, built in the Russian-controlled area to avoid Prussian territory.

The Masurian Lakes provide around 200km of navigable waters with several locks and short canals connecting them. It was long the desire of Prussia to connect the lakes to the rest of the navigable waterways of

A passenger boat on the Masurian Lakes system which is extensively used for pleasure.

The remains of one of the unfinished locks on the Masurian Canal.

the area, and in 1874 the plan for the Masurian Canal was published. Work on the canal, which was to run northwards for 50km, reaching Königsberg (Kaliningrad) by the river system, began in 1908. It was never completed because of the First World War, but work on a new scheme began again in 1934, but this too remains unfinished, victim to the Second World War.

After the Second World War, waterway traffic has been mainly restricted to the Oder, the Bydgoszcz Canal system and the lower Vistula. Since the end of Communism, apart from the heavily used lower Oder, most commercial traffic has ceased. However, the smaller Elblag and Augustowski canals and the Masurian Lakes are being used increasingly by pleasure boats.

Images of the Odra in the 1950s

Photographs by

Mieczysław Wróblewski

*The reflection of the steam tug **Śląsk** (**Silesia**), photographed whilst waiting for work in the Osobowice 1 Harbour, in 1960.*

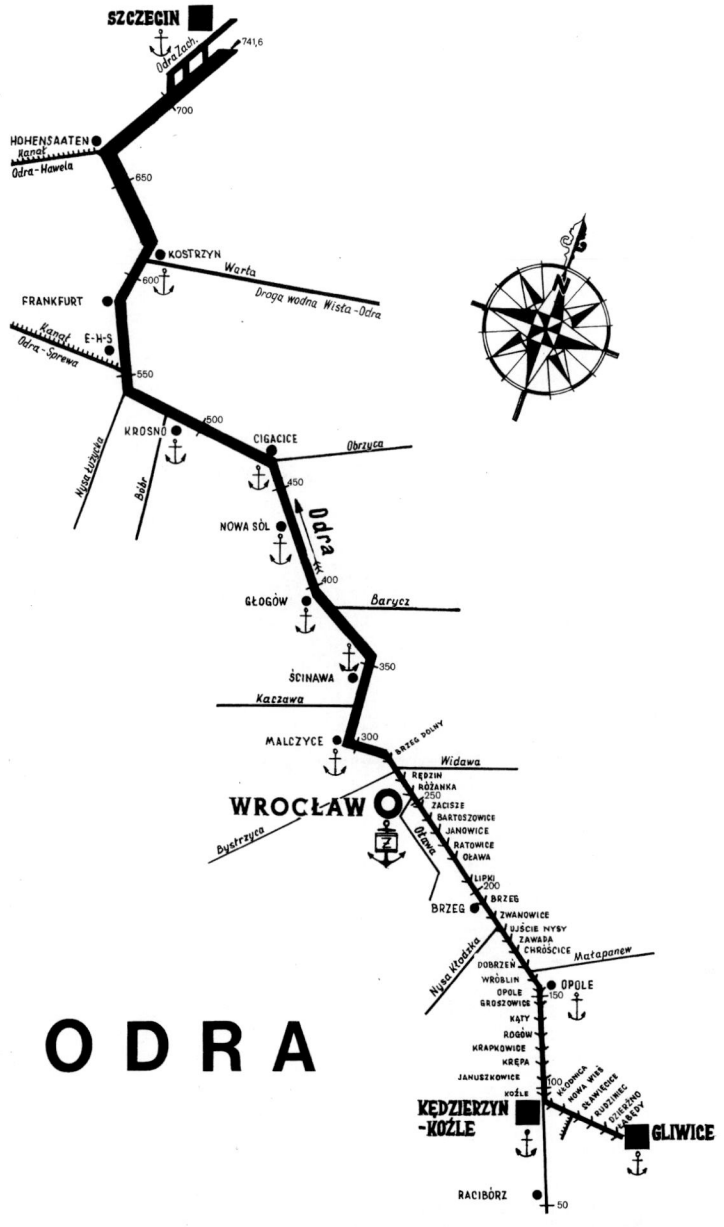

Retired lieutenant commander Mieczysław Wróblewski (born in 1916), who took these photographs, has been connected with maritime and navigation affairs since 1935. A graduate of the Polish Military Maritime Officer Cadet School, in September 1939 he fought in the Gdańsk Gulf on ORP **Rybitwa**. On returning from captivity, he commanded a minesweeper division and taught young military officers. From 1953 until 1981 he worked on the Odra River in Wrocław, managing the Inland Navigation Inspectorate. Today he is retired and co-operates with the Foundation for the Open Museum of Technology. Thanks to his love of the river, they have a collection of 5,000 photographs of life and work on the Odra. These are just a small sample of the wonderful images he took.

A map of the Oder, including the Gliwice Canal. The small branch from the canal was to have been the start of the Oder-Danube Canal.

*The steam tug **Śląsk**, 1956.*

The steam tug **Dolny Śląsk** (*Lower Silesia*), 1957.

*The steam tug **Mieszko 1**, 20th April 1957.*

*The paddle tug **Kędzierzyn**, 1956.*

In the wheelhouse of a towed barge, May 1954.

*Captain Reinhold Sapok's family, including the twins, being brought up on the tug **Karkonosze**, 1956.*

Dad keeping an eye on his son, 1956.

Szymura, the engineer in the engine room of the tug **Jarowid**, one of the 'Large Dutchmen', in 1956.

*The tug **Swiatopełk**, one of the 'Small Dutchmen', and its crew when passing through a lock 1956.*

In the Różanka Lock in Wrocław, 1956. The lock has a segment gate which is lifted upwards by rotation for the boats to pass underneath.

Inset: The unusual lock gate opening mechanism.

A hardworking horse of the river, the Odra at Krapkowice, near Opole, 19th September, 1958. The tug is one of the 'Little Dutchmen', which were supplied by Holland after the Second World War.

The **Swiatopełk**, a 'Small Dutchman', and the **Radgost**, a 'Large Dutchman', recovering a barge, damaged by the river bed, 1956. The shallowness of the river was a particular problem in summer.

Barges in the winter harbour, Osobowice I, 1955/56. When the river was frozen, all boats were kept away from the main channel which had to be free so that ice did not form a dam and cause flooding.

Inset: Breaking the ice around the boats to prevent them being crushed. The boatman on the left is using a special saw to cut the ice.

The passenger boat **Zeromski**, passing under the Grunwaldski Bridge in Wrocław, May 1955. 'Most Grunwaldzki' or the Kaiser Bridge was opened on 10th October 1910. As originally built, the towers were slightly higher, but towards the end of the Second World War, the road to the north of the bridge was converted into a runway by the Germans and the tops were removed to make take-off and landing easier.

Boatmen everywhere kept chickens!

Sponsors of the exhibition include:
The General Conservator of Monuments of the Republic of Poland, Warszawa.
Foundation for the Open Museum of Technology, Wrocław.
Technical Monument Study & Documentation Office, Wrocław.
HOBAS Poland Ltd, Poznan.

Hydroprojekt Ltd, Wrocław.
ODRATRANS SA, Wrocław.
Regional Management of Water Administration in Wrocław.
TAN SA. Engineering and Hydrotechnology Enterprise, Wrocław.
Milepost Research, Accrington.
The Waterways Trust, National Waterways Museum.

The **Nadbór** is the last surviving Odra steam tug and it is being restored as a museum-ship. There is a lecture room and exhibition space for the Foundation for the Open Museum of Technology (FOMT) and for courses on industrial history run by the nearby Polytechnic.

Moored in central Wrocław, an exhibition on the embankment alongside is proposed for the display a variety of historical equipment connected with the Odra River, such as items used in harbours, shipyards and on boats, as well as flood prevention controls, and environmental equipment concerned with water quality etc.

In July 1998, the historic steam tug **Nadbór** became the office for the Technical Monument Study & Documentation Centre, a business undertaking the recording of technical monuments, teaching historical & conservatory studies and involved with all aspects of industrial & technical heritage. It has its own computer data base covering over 7,000 industrial & technical monuments in Poland, including some 50,000 photos and about 10,000 drawings.